Senses

KINGFISHER

Published in 2010 by Kingfisher
an imprint of Macmillan Children's Books
a division of Macmillan Publishers Limited
20 New Wharf Road
London N1 9RR
Basingstoke and Oxford
Associated companies throughout the world
www.panmacmillan.com

ISBN 978-0-7534-3003-3

First published as *Kingfisher Young Knowledge: Senses* in 2004
Additional material produced for Macmillan Children's Books by Discovery Books Ltd

1 3 5 7 9 8 6 4 2

1TR/0410/WKT/UNTD/140MA/C

A CIP catalogue record for this book is available from the British Library.

Printed in China

Note to readers: the website addresses listed in this book are correct at
the time of going to print. However, due to the ever-changing nature
of the internet, website addresses and content can change. Websites
can contain links that are unsuitable for children. The publisher cannot
be held responsible for changes in website addresses or content, or
for information obtained through a third party. We strongly advise
that internet searches should be supervised by an adult.

Acknowledgements

The publishers would like to thank the following for permission to reproduce their material. Every care has been taken
to trace copyright holders. However, if there have been unintentional omissions or failure to trace copyright holders,
we apologize and will, if informed, endeavour to make corrections in any future edition.
b = bottom, *c* = centre, *l* = left, *t* = top, *r* = right

Cover main Shutterstock/Rick Becker-Leckrone; cover *l* Shutterstock/Renata Osinka; cover *r* Shutterstock/Andriy Petrenko; 1 Corbis; 2–3 Michael K. Nichols/National
Geographic; 4–5 Raymond Gehman/National Geographic; 6–7 Alamy Images; 9*r* Digital Vision; 10*cl* Adam Hart-Davis/Science Photo Library; 10–11*b* Sean
Murphy/Getty Images; 12*l* Piers Cavendish/ardea.com; 12–13*t* DiMaggio/Kalish/Corbis; 13*br* Jeff Lepore/Science Photo Library; 14*bl* NHPA/James Carmichael Jr;
14–15*tc* NHPA/Stephen Dalton; 15*br* NHPA/Nigel J Dennis; 17*br* Susumu Nishinaga/Science Photo Library; 18*l* Mark Baker/Reuters; 18–19*b* Roy Morsch/Corbis;
19*tr* Tony Marshall/EMPICS Sports Photo Agency; 20*l* NHPA/William Paton; 20–21*c* NHPA/Daryl Balfour; 21*br* Duncan McEwan/Nature Picture Library; 22*bl(l)* Joel
W. Rogers/Corbis; 22*bl(r)* Nick Gordon/ardea.com; 22–23*t* NHPA/ANT Photo Library; 23*br* Georgettte Douwma/Getty Images; 24*bl* NHPA/Stephen Dalton;
25*tr* NHPA/ANT Photo Library; 25*br* Dietmar Nill/Nature Picture Library; 26*l* Craig Hammel/Corbis; 27*br* BSIP VEM/Science Photo Library; 27*br* Suzanne & Nick
Geary/Getty Images; 28*tl* François Gohier/ardea.com; 28–29*b* NHPA/Guy Edwardes; 29*tr* NHPA/Ann & Steve Toon; 30–31*b* Pascal Goetgheluck/ardea.com;
31*tr* John Downer Productions/Nature Picture Library; 31*br* Roy Morsch/Corbis; 32*br* Corbis; 33*b* Omikron/Science Photo Library; 34*l* NHPA/Martin Harvey; 34–35*b*
NHPA/T Kitchin & V Hurst; 35*tr* Matthew Oldfield, Scubazoo/Science Photo Library; 37*tl* Phil Jude/Science Photo Library; 38*l* Angelo Cavalli/Getty Images and Ryan
Mcvay/Getty Images; 38–39*b* NHPA/Kevin Schafer; 39*tr* Dr Jeremy Burgess/Science Photo Library; 48*c* Shutterstock Images/ultimathule; 48*b* Shutterstock
Images/Vasiliy Koval; 49*t* Shutterstock Images/Kruglov_Orda; 49*b* Shutterstock Images/Andrew Armyagov; 52*c* Shutterstock Images/orionmystery@flickr;
52*b* Shutterstock Images/Eric Isselée; 53*c* Shutterstock Images/Annamaria Szilagyi; 53*b* Shutterstock Images/EcoPrint; 56*t* Shutterstock Images/Eric Isselée

Commissioned photography on pages 33, 36 and 42–47 by Andy Crawford
Thank you to models Corey Addai, Anastasia Mitchell, Sonnie Nash and Shannon Porter

Senses

Jinny Johnson

KINGFISHER

Contents

What are senses?

Imagine the world if you could not see things or hear your friends talking, or if you could not smell and taste your food. We do not often think about our senses, but they tell us what is going on around us. We have five main senses. These are sight, hearing, smell, taste and touch.

Super senses

Animals have senses too. Some animals have better senses than we do. Dogs can hear sounds that humans cannot, and they have a much stronger sense of smell.

Using senses

This boy can see his pet's big brown eyes, feel his soft fur and hear his snuffling sounds. He can also smell the roses in the background and can probably smell his dog.

The sense centre

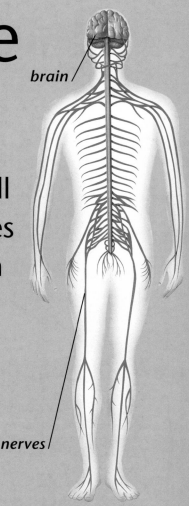

brain

nerves

Your brain controls your senses. Messages travel from your eyes, ears, nose, tongue and skin to tell it what is going on. The messages travel along special pathways in the body called nerves.

Messages to the brain

Nerves go from the brain to all parts of your body. A message can zoom along the nerves to the brain in a tiny fraction of a second.

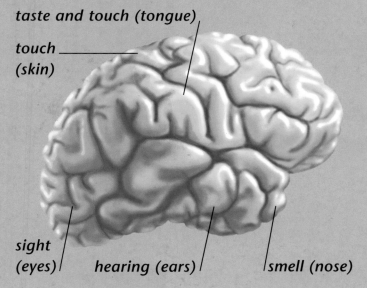

taste and touch (tongue)

touch (skin)

sight (eyes)

hearing (ears)

smell (nose)

Jobs for the brain

The brain sorts out the messages it receives from the nerves. Look at the picture on the left to see which parts of the brain sort out messages to do with your senses.

brain

Keeping your brain safe

Your brain is inside your head. Feel your bony skull at the top of your head. It protects your brain. Your brain is usually fully grown by the time you are about six years old.

How do I see?

Your eyes make pictures of the outside world – a bit like a camera does. You can see big things and small things, and you can see lots of different colours.

pupil (black)

iris (brown)

Letting in light

The black circle at the centre of your eye is called the pupil. This is an opening through which light passes into your eye.

Eye colour

The coloured part of the eye is called the iris. It can be blue, green or brown. What colour irises do these children have?

Making a picture

When you look at something, light bounces off it and goes into your eye. Inside the eye the lens makes an image on the area called the retina, at the back of the eye. Messages about this image travel along nerves to the brain.

iris

pupil

lens

retina

nerves

bone in eye socket

Amazing eyesight

Some animals have excellent eyesight. Their eyes need to be right for the job they have to do – such as spotting food or looking out for danger.

Night eyes

Hunting animals, such as this cat, have powerful, forward-facing eyes that help them see detail well and judge exactly where something is. Cats can see much better at night than we can.

Sharp sight

Birds of prey, such as this peregrine falcon, can see things from a long way away. Its large, alert eyes can spy a tiny mouse from high up in the air.

All-round view

Side-facing eyes help this
mouse see as much of what
is going on around it as
possible. This means it can
spot any enemies – and
has a chance to escape!

Different eyes

Not all animals have eyes quite like ours. Some animals have eyes that look very different, but are perfect for helping them find food.

Spider eyes

Most spiders have eight eyes. But only the two large eyes at the front are used for seeing. The smaller ones pick out any movement and help the main eyes find prey.

Two directions

The chameleon stays very still as it watches for insects to catch. Its big, bulgy eyes can swivel around and even point in two directions at once.

LEA			

This item is to be returned or renewed before the latest date above. It may be borrowed for a further period if not in demand. **To renew your books:**

- **Phone the 24/7 Renewal Line 01926 499273 or**
- **Visit www.warwickshire.gov.uk/libraries**

Discover • Imagine • Learn • *with libraries*

Warwickshire
County Council

Working for Warwickshire

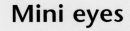

Mini eyes

A dragonfly's eye is made up of 30,000 parts. Each one is like a tiny eye. These let the dragonfly see lots of images at high speed so it can track fast-moving prey.

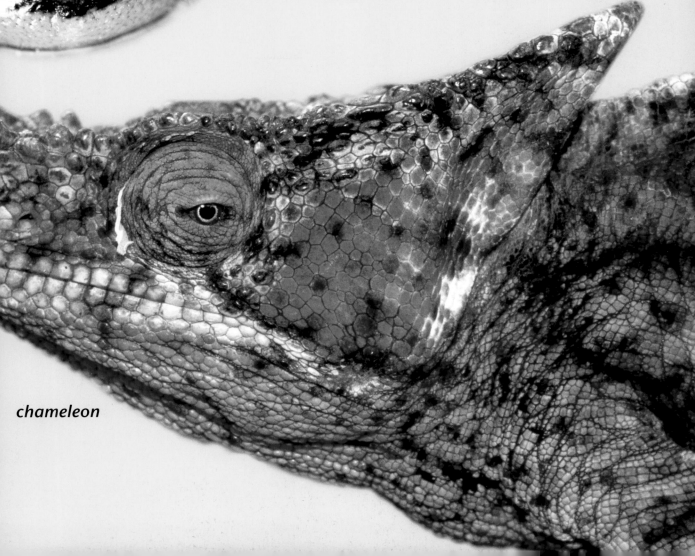

chameleon

How do I hear?

Your ears allow you to hear sounds, from a quiet whisper to the loudest pop music. The outside parts of your ears pick up sounds and funnel them down inside your ears.

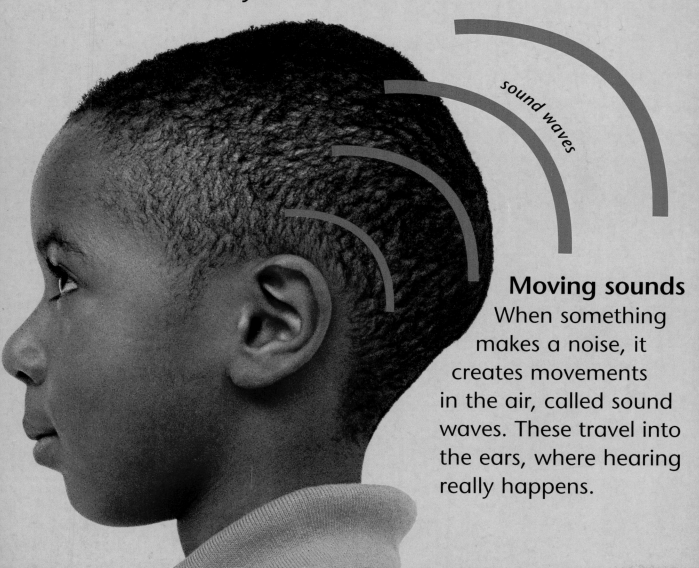

sound waves

Moving sounds
When something makes a noise, it creates movements in the air, called sound waves. These travel into the ears, where hearing really happens.

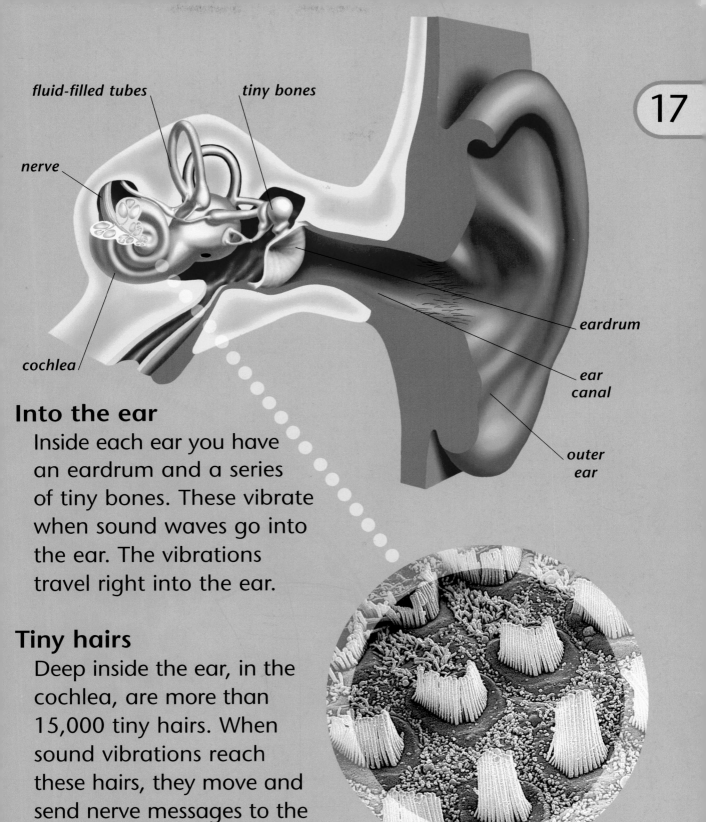

fluid-filled tubes

tiny bones

nerve

cochlea

eardrum

ear canal

outer ear

Into the ear

Inside each ear you have an eardrum and a series of tiny bones. These vibrate when sound waves go into the ear. The vibrations travel right into the ear.

Tiny hairs

Deep inside the ear, in the cochlea, are more than 15,000 tiny hairs. When sound vibrations reach these hairs, they move and send nerve messages to the brain – and you hear.

Keeping balanced

As well as allowing you to hear sounds, your ears help you to keep your balance. As you move around, tiny hairs in fluid-filled tubes in your ear tell you which way up you are.

Travel sick

You may feel sick on a boat because your brain gets confused. Your ears tell it you are moving but your eyes say you are not.

Dizzy spells

If you spin around, then suddenly stop, your ears do not get the message to your brain straight away. You feel this as dizziness.

Practice makes perfect

Gymnasts do not get dizzy because they practise their moves over and over again so that their brains get used to the signals.

Animal ears

Ears come in all shapes and sizes. The ears of the African elephant are the biggest of all. They can be two metres long.

Listening for danger

The rabbit's long ears help it catch the tiniest sound that might mean danger is near. It can also swivel its ears to pick up sounds from different directions.

Far-away calls

Elephants can hear much deeper sounds than we can. They can hear the low calls of other elephants from several kilometres away.

Insect ears

Some insects have ears in surprising places. Crickets have ears on their front legs. This grasshopper has its ears on each side of its body.

Listening underwater

The ocean may look like a silent world, but it is not. Sounds travel further through water than air, and fish, whales and other creatures can hear sounds.

Closed ears

An otter does not use its ears underwater. When it dives, it closes its ears so it will not get water in them.

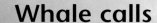

Whale calls

All you can see of a whale's ears is a tiny hole on each side of its head. But whales have excellent hearing. A humpback whale can hear the calls of other whales from many kilometres away.

humpback whale

Listening fish

Fish have ears inside their bodies that allow them to hear what is going on around them. They make noises to keep in touch with each other and listen for sounds of enemies – or food!

Sound pictures

Bats, whales and dolphins are some of the creatures that have a special sense called echolocation. This means that they use sound instead of sight to make a 'picture' of their surroundings.

Night hunters

Bats hunt at night and can catch an insect in total darkness by using echolocation. As it flies, the bat makes lots of very high sounds. . .

'Seeing' sounds

Echolocation works in water, too. Dolphins find food in the deep, dark ocean by making sounds that echo and help them 'see' their prey.

Sound echoes

. . . When the bat's sounds meet an insect, they make echoes that bounce back to the bat's ears. The echoes tell the bat where its prey is, how big it is and even how fast it is moving.

Smelling things

Your sense of smell happens inside your nose. Most of the outside of your nose is to do with warming and cleaning the air you breathe in before it travels to your lungs.

A-tishoo!

You sneeze when something irritates the inside of your nose and your body tries to force it out. The tiny hairs in your nose trap dust and dirt, and stop it getting into your lungs.

How you smell

When you smell something, tiny bits of its scent travel into your nose. They go right to the top into two special sense areas. Nerves send messages from there to your brain, telling it about the smell.

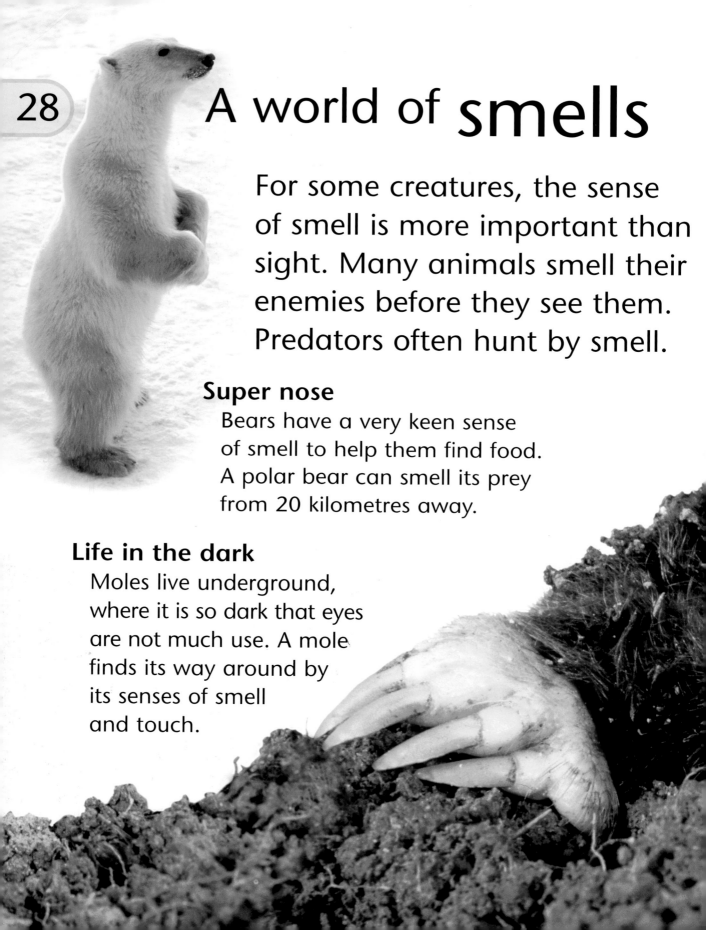

A world of smells

For some creatures, the sense of smell is more important than sight. Many animals smell their enemies before they see them. Predators often hunt by smell.

Super nose

Bears have a very keen sense of smell to help them find food. A polar bear can smell its prey from 20 kilometres away.

Life in the dark

Moles live underground, where it is so dark that eyes are not much use. A mole finds its way around by its senses of smell and touch.

Smell check

Deer take a break now and then from feeding on grass, and look up to sniff the air for any signs of danger.

Smelly messages

Many animals use smell to send messages to each other. These might say 'Keep away' or 'I am looking for a mate.' When a dog sniffs a tree it can tell which other dogs have marked the spot.

Special signals

When a female moth is ready to mate she gives off a special scent. The feathery antennae on a male moth's head can pick up the smell from five kilometres away.

Smelly warning

The skunk uses smell to protect itself. If an enemy comes too close, the skunk squirts out a very smelly liquid from an area near its tail, to warn it off.

My mark

When a cat rubs its cheeks against something, it is leaving a scent message. It is saying 'I was here. This is my patch.'

Tasting things

Your sense of taste works with your sense of smell to tell you about the food you eat. You taste with your tongue. Taste helps you enjoy food, but also warns you if something is not good to eat.

Four flavours

There are four main flavours: bitter, salty, sour and sweet. Most foods are a mixture of more than one of these. Different areas of the tongue are sensitive to certain flavours. Match the colours below to the picture opposite to see where these are.

bitter *salty*

sour *sweet*

Taste buds

Your tongue is covered with about 10,000 tiny taste buds, which are too small to see. Each taste bud is sensitive to a particular kind of taste.

Bumpy tongue

Your taste buds are clustered around the little bumps you can see on your tongue. Nerves inside the taste buds send messages to your brain about what you are tasting.

Animal tastes

Like us, animals have taste buds on their tongues, but it is hard to know just what they taste. Most probably use smell and taste to tell what is good to eat.

Good taste

Tigers – and pet cats – have sensitive tongues. They can taste different flavours in ordinary water.

Swimming tongues

Catfish are like swimming tongues – they have taste buds on their bodies, which help them find food in the water. They can also taste food with their whiskers, called barbels.

Tasting toes

Butterflies taste with their feet as well as with their mouths. This way, they know what kind of food they have landed on before they unroll their tongues to eat.

Touch and feel

soft

You can feel with any part of your body because your skin contains lots of tiny nerve endings. These send messages to the brain about what you are touching.

What does it feel like?

When you hold something, notice how it feels. It may be rough or smooth, sharp or soft, hot or cold. Our sense of touch tells us these things. It also lets us feel pain.

cold

hot

sharp

smooth

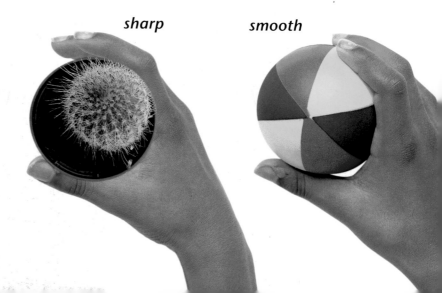

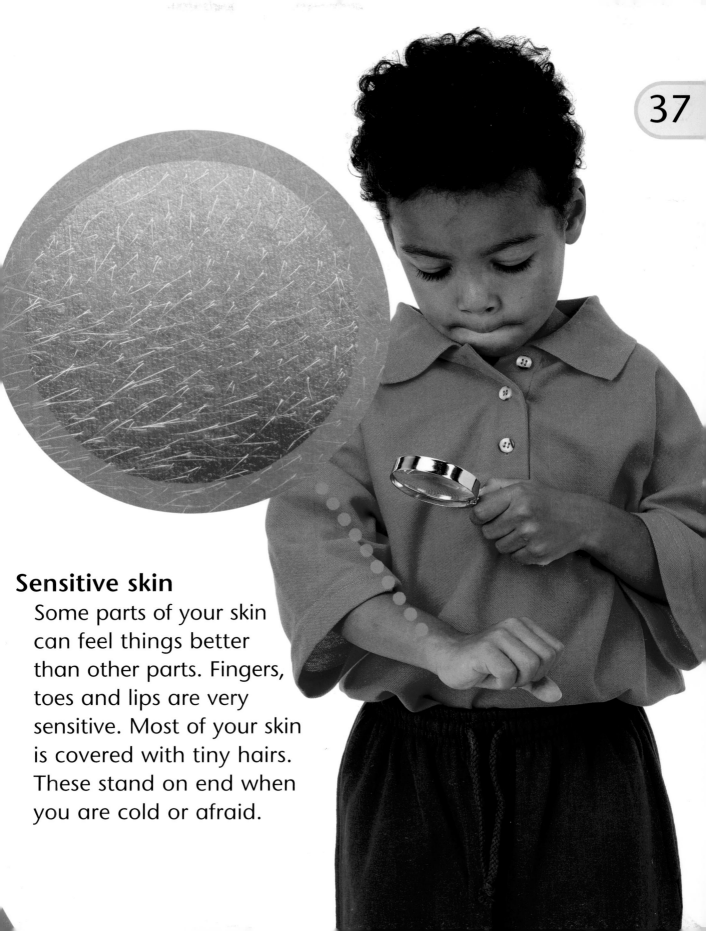

Sensitive skin

Some parts of your skin
can feel things better
than other parts. Fingers,
toes and lips are very
sensitive. Most of your skin
is covered with tiny hairs.
These stand on end when
you are cold or afraid.

Animal **touch**

Animals feel things with their skin too. But some have extra ways of touching. Many animals have very sensitive whiskers, which help them find out about their surroundings.

Super trunk
The tip of an elephant's trunk is the most sensitive part of its body. It does lots of things with its trunk, from stroking its young to picking up tiny leaves.

Hairy legs

A spider waits on its web for its prey. Hairs on the spider's legs sense the tiniest movement that might mean food is near.

Wet paws

The raccoon has very sensitive paws as well as whiskers. They are even more sensitive when wet, which may be why the raccoon wets its paws before eating.

Which line is longer?
Seeing involves your brain as well as your eyes. Sometimes your brain can be tricked into seeing something that is not really there.

Using your ruler, draw a straight line 9cm long. Draw another 9cm line beside the first line, about 5cm away.

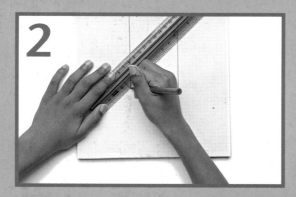

On the first line, draw arrowheads pointing outwards. On the second line, draw arrowheads pointing inwards, as shown in step 3.

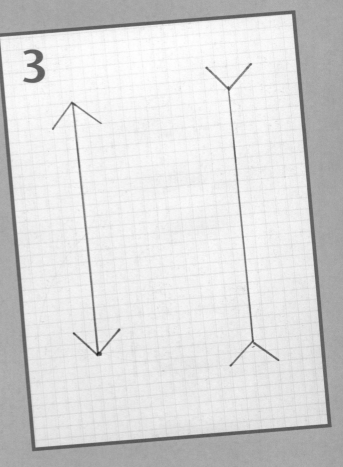

Look at the straight lines. Does one look longer than the other? The directions of the arrowheads trick your brain into thinking that one line is longer than the other.

Hole in the hand

Trick your eyes

Your brain can get confused if your two eyes see two different images. The brain puts the images together and this can create a strange picture, like this illusion where you seem to see a hole in your hand.

1 Hold a cardboard tube up to your right eye. Then hold up your left hand next to the tube, with the palm towards you.

2 Look straight ahead. Your right eye should be looking through the tube and your left eye at your palm. Can you see a hole in your hand? Your eyes are playing tricks on your brain.

Model eardrum

How hearing works

Make a loud noise and you will see the stretched balloon on your model eardrum vibrate just like your real eardrum does.

You will need
- Balloon
- Scissors
- Plastic cup
- Elastic band
- Rice grains

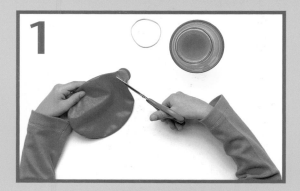

Use scissors to cut the neck off a balloon. Then carefully cut down one side so that you can open the balloon out flat.

Cut the opened-out balloon in half so you have a piece big enough to fit over the top of your plastic cup. This will be the eardrum itself.

Stretch the balloon over the cup. Fix it on with the elastic band, keeping the balloon stretched as tightly as possible.

Sprinkle some rice grains on top of the balloon. Clap your hands or shout. Watch the grains jump as the stretched balloon vibrates.

Listening game

What can you hear?
Find a quiet spot and play this game – you will be surprised at the number of different sounds you hear.

You will need
- Notepad
- Pen

Sit down with your notepad and pen. Listen carefully for sounds – a noisy lorry, birds singing or a dog barking. Write down or draw pictures of the things you hear.

Taste and smell

Guess the smell

You will be surprised at how difficult it is to tell what things are without looking at them, using just your sense of smell.

Ask a friend to sit down, and tie a scarf over his eyes. Make sure it is tight enough that he cannot see, but not so tight that it hurts.

Add one smelly thing to each plastic cup. Then hold the first cup under your friend's nose and ask him to take a good sniff.

Ask him to smell and guess what is in the cup.

Give him the other foods to smell one by one. See how many he can get right. Some smells are easy to guess, while others are harder.

Guess the taste

Try guessing different drinks by taste alone. It can be difficult when you cannot see them, especially if some are similar.

You will need
- Scarf
- 5 plastic cups
- 5 drinks: we used milk, chocolate milk, orange juice, apple juice and water

1

As with the smelling game, ask a friend to sit down, and tie a scarf over her eyes. Make sure she is comfortable but cannot see.

2

Pour five different drinks into the plastic cups. Make sure you ask an adult which drinks you can use.

3

Ask your friend to take a sip of the first drink and guess what it is. Ask her to try each in turn, and see how many she gets right.

Make a touch cube

Test your touch

This is a fun way to test your sense of touch. When you have made the cube, you can play with it or play a touch guessing game.

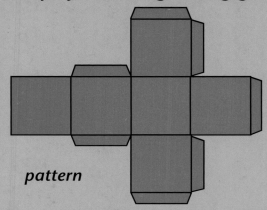

pattern

To make your touch cube you will need to cut a piece of card in the pattern shown above. You might need to ask an adult to help you copy it.

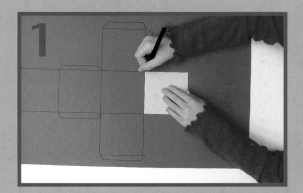

1

Place your card square on the stiff card. Draw around it six times to make the pattern. Add flaps where shown in the pattern.

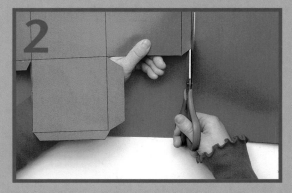

2

Carefully cut around the outside of the pattern, keeping all the edges as straight as you can. Then fold along all the lines.

3

Hold the middle square down with your finger and fold up the sides to make a box shape. Glue down the flaps to stick the box together.

4

Take some cereal shapes and carefully glue them to one side of the box to make a rough texture. You can use any kind you like.

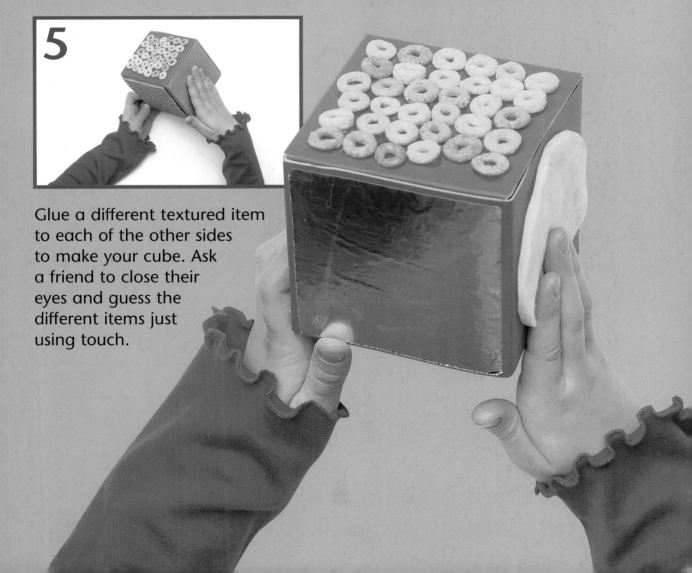

5

Glue a different textured item to each of the other sides to make your cube. Ask a friend to close their eyes and guess the different items just using touch.

Glossary

Alert – if you are alert you are paying attention to what is going on around you

Antenna – a feeler on an insect's head

Balance – the ability to keep upright and not fall over

Brain – the organ inside your head that controls your body and allows you to think and have feelings

Camera – a machine used for taking photographs

Clustered – to be in a crowd, close together

Confused – if you are confused, you don't understand something

Echo – a sound that bounces off an object

Enemy – something that wants to harm or eat you

Escape – to break free from a place where you have been kept by force

Eyesight – the ability to see

Flavour – taste

Fraction – a small amount

Funnel – to direct something through a narrow space

Gymnast – someone who is trained and skilled in gymnastics

Image – a picture

Irritate – if something irritates you, it causes you discomfort

Lens – part of the eye that focuses light

Lungs – two large, spongy bags in your chest that you use for breathing

Nerves – special structures like wires that run from the brain to all parts of the body

Ordinary – normal

Predator – an animal that hunts and eats other animals

Prey – an animal that is killed or eaten by another animal

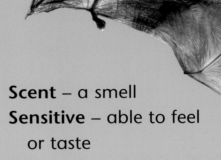

Scent – a smell

Sensitive – able to feel or taste

Signal – an action, sound or gesture used to give a message to someone

Skull – the bony part of your head that protects your brain

Surroundings – the area and environment around you

Swivel – to turn around on the spot

Vibrate – to move rapidly to and fro

Whiskers – long hairs on an animal's face

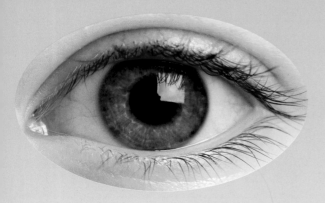

This book includes material that would be particularly useful in helping to teach children aged 7–11. It covers many elements of the English and Science curricula and provides opportunities for cross-curricular lessons, especially those involving Geography and Art.

Extension activities:

Writing
Each double-page information spread has a title, introduction and three paragraphs of text, each with its own sub-heading.

1) This book is about the five senses. What could a sixth sense be? What would it do?

2) See the cross-curricular suggestions for ideas on writing reports and poetry based on the senses.

Speaking and listening
Ask five children or groups each to think about a different sense. They must find reasons why it is the most important sense. Then hold a class discussion.

Science
1) Choose an animal and decide which senses it uses least and most. Why?

2) Make a pinhole camera to show how light travels in straight lines.

3) Find five different animals with side-facing eyes. Can you find one for each grouping: mammals, reptiles, fish, amphibians and birds?

4) To see sound waves in action, hold a tissue near a big bass speaker – the music creates vibrations in the air that move the tissue.

5) Use a medicine dropper to put small amounts of salted water, sugared water, lemon juice and sour milk on different parts of your tongue. Where did each taste strongest?

Cross-curricular links
1) *History:* Describe a time in history, such as ancient Egypt or life during World War II. Using only one of the senses, write about

what you might see, or hear, or smell or touch. Can you turn your writing into a riddle or a poem?

2) Geography: Apply this idea of using only one sense to describe places such as a beach, playground or a busy market. Now try this with habitats such as the desert, rainforest or an animal's underground burrow.

Using the projects
Children can follow or adapt these projects at home. Here are some ideas for extending them:

Page 40: Can you make up or find other optical illusions using dots, circles or lines?

Page 41: Point your index fingers together, not quite touching, about 10 centimetres in front of your eyes. Look past them to focus on the opposite wall. Do you see a floating sausage shape? Move your fingers apart and together to change the length of the 'sausage'. Your eyes are playing tricks on you again!

Pages 42–43: Play the 'listening game' in the same location but at different times of the day and night. How do your lists of sounds compare?

Pages 44–45: Make the task harder by offering two foods at the same time. Can you identify them both? You can take this activity a little further. Still using the blindfold, have the taster hold his or her nose while tasting each of the five liquids. How does our sense of smell influence our sense of taste?

Page 46: Make a second cube with textures that are similar to each other, such as felt, velvet and fur. With practice, does it get easier to tell them apart?

Did you know?

- Most adult humans can tell the difference between about 10,000 different smells.

- The giant anteater has the longest tongue in relation to its body size of any mammal.

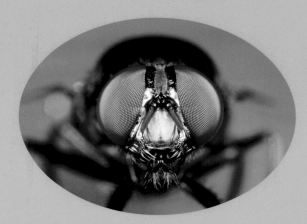

- Butterflies have hairs on their wings which detect changes in air pressure.

- Earthworms have taste buds all over their bodies. They use these to sense their surroundings.

- Camels have three eyelids. The first two have very long lashes to stop sand getting in their eyes. Their third eyelid is clear so the camel can see during a sandstorm.

- Worker bees have 5,500 lenses in each eye.

- A buzzard can see small rodents from a height of 4,500 metres.

- Many crabs have their eyes on the ends of stalks.

- Bluebottle flies taste with 3,000 sensory hairs on their feet.

- A box jellyfish has 24 eyes!

- Some people cannot tell the difference between red colours and green colours. They are said to be colour blind.

- Fingertips are full of nerve endings. People who are blind can use their sense of touch to read Braille, a kind of writing that uses a series of raised dots to represent different letters of the alphabet.

- A newborn baby sees the world upside down because it takes some time for the baby's brain to learn to turn the picture the correct way up.

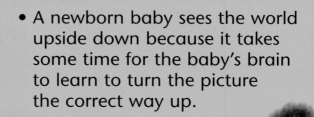

- Most people blink every 2–10 seconds.

- Dogs have 1 million smell cells per nostril. Their smell cells are 100 times larger than a human's.

- You have more pain nerve endings than any other type.

- The least sensitive part of your body is the middle of your back.

- Shivering is the way your body tries to keep warm.

- An earache is caused by too much fluid putting pressure on your eardrum. Earaches are often the result of an infection, allergies or a virus.

Senses quiz

The answers to these questions can all be found by looking back through the book. See how many you get right. You can check your answers on page 56.

1) How many main senses do we have?
   A – Three
   B – Four
   C – Five

2) What controls our senses?
   A – Brain
   B – Muscles
   C – Heart

3) What is the black circle in the centre of the eye called?
   A – Pupil
   B – Iris
   C – Retina

4) A dragonfly's eye is made up of...
   A – 4,000 parts
   B – 30,000 parts
   C – 1,000 parts

5) Why might you feel sick on a boat?
   A – Your brain gets confused
   B – Your eyes get confused
   C – Your legs get confused

6) Crickets have ears on their...
   A – Tongue
   B – Back
   C – Front legs

7) When do bats hunt?
   A – At night
   B – In the morning
   C – Just after lunchtime

8) What does a female moth do when she is ready to mate?
   A – Makes a high-pitched noise
   B – Gives off a special scent
   C – Dances

9) How many main flavours are there?
   A – Three
   B – Four
   C – Five

10) Butterflies have tongues but what do they also use to taste?
   A – Nose
   B – Wings
   C – Feet

11) What is the most sensitive part of an elephant's body?
   A – Ears
   B – Trunk
   C – Tail

12) What happens to the hairs on your skin when you are afraid?
   A – They grow more quickly
   B – They lie flat
   C – They stand on end

Books to read

Body Science: The Senses by Rufus Bellamy, Franklin Watts, 2004

I Wonder Why Lemons Taste Sour and other questions about senses by Deborah Chancellor, Kingfisher, 2007

The Kingfisher Book of the Human Body by Dr Patricia Macnair, Kingfisher, 2005

My Amazing Body: Senses by Angela Royston, Raintree, 2004

Understanding the Human Body: Senses by Carol Ballard, Wayland, 2009

What Happens When You Use Your Senses? by Jacqui Bailey, Wayland, 2007

Places to visit

Science Museum, London
www.sciencemuseum.org.uk
Visit the fascinating IMAX three-dimensional cinema. Find out about how all of our senses work with exhibitions and online exercises, too.

Natural History Museum, London
www.nhm.ac.uk
Learn about the secret world of bats. Find out how bats use their senses to hunt for food, find their way back home and keep out of harm's way.

Eureka! The National Children's Museum, Halifax
www.eureka.org.uk
Learn about how your body works in this hands-on learning environment. Learn about your five senses and how they work with a giant nose, tongue, ear and eye to help you. Find the feely boxes to discover what your hands and fingers tell you.

Birmingham Science Museum
www.culture24.org.uk/ am10462?id=EDR28837
Learn about the five senses with a one-hour workshop. Find out where your sensory organs are and how you use them through role play and group discussions.

Websites

www.bbc.co.uk/science/humanbody/ body/
Click on the Nervous System section. This contains information, animations and quizzes about human senses.

dsc.discovery.com/tv/human-body/ explorer/explorer.html
Interactive website with activities such as putting the correct pieces together to build your own three-dimensional eye!

http://faculty.washington.edu/chudler/ introb.html
An interesting website with information, activities, games and quizzes about the nervous system and senses.

Senses quiz answers

1) C	7) A
2) A	8) B
3) A	9) B
4) B	10) C
5) A	11) B
6) C	12) C